NANA, I WANT TO HEAR YOUR STORY

SECTION ONE
THE BEGINNING

SECTION TWO
FAMILY HISTORY

SECTION THREE
CHILDHOOD YEARS

SECTION FOUR
TEENAGE YEARS

SECTION FIVE
WHEN I WAS..

SECTION SIX
PARENTHOOD

SECTION SIX
MORE ABOUT ME!

SECTION SEVEN
FINAL NOTES

©The Life Graduate Publishing Group
www.thelifegraduate.com

No part of this book may be scanned, reproduced or distributed in any printed or electronic form without the prior permission of the author or publisher.

Created by Romney Nelson

A Place to Share My Life Memories.

Love Nana xx

"Mother is the name for God in the lips and hearts of little children."
— William Makepeace Thackeray

THIS IS THE BEGINNING...

Baby Nana

MY INTRODUCTION

Before I start....Just a brief introduction of me!

_____
_____
_____
_____
_____
_____
_____
_____

Name:

Signature

Date

THE BEGINNING.....

Full Name at Birth
_____

Date of Birth   / /
_____

Time of Birth   :
_____

Day of the week you were born?
_____

Height at birth? (if known)
_____

Weight at birth? (If known)
_____

Your Place of Birth (include the City/Town, Country)
_____

Did you have any siblings when you were born? If so, what were their names and their ages?

_____

_____

_____

ADD ANY ADDITIONAL NOTES OR INFORMATION HERE...

THE BEGINNING.....

Share with us some information about your parents?

_____

_____

_____

_____

_____

Were you in good health as a baby?

_____

_____

Did you have any unique characteristics or funny things you did as a baby?

_____

_____

_____

IF YOU HAVE ANY EARLY BABY PHOTOS, INCLUDE THEM HERE...

THE BEGINNING.....

Were you an active or quiet baby?
_____

Were you ever told what your first words were?
_____
_____

Do you have any other baby memories to share?
_____
_____
_____
_____
_____
_____

"There is no influence so powerful as that of a mother."
—Sara Josepha Hale

FAMILY HISTORY

This is our Family Tree!

FAMILY HISTORY

My grandparents names were:

Grandmother: _____

Grandfather: _____

They were born in: (country)
Grandmother: _____

Grandfather: _____

This is something that not many people may know about our family history……

_____
_____
_____
_____
_____

Additional Family History information:

_____
_____
_____

Our FAMILY TREE

Grandfather

Grandfather

Grandmother

Grandmother

Mother

Father

Me

ADD ANY ADDITIONAL NOTES OR INFORMATION HERE...

CHILDHOOD YEARS

CHILDHOOD YEARS....

What was your favorite toy growing up?

_____
_____

Did you have a pet or any pets growing up?

_____
_____

What was your favorite T.V show to watch as a child?

_____
_____

Was there a moment you remember getting into big trouble as a child? Was there a punishment?

_____
_____
_____
_____
_____

ADD ANY ADDITIONAL NOTES OR INFORMATION HERE...

CHILDHOOD YEARS....

What are your fondest memories growing up between the ages of 5 - 12 years?

_____
_____
_____
_____
_____
_____
_____
_____
_____
_____
_____
_____

IF YOU HAVE ANY EARLY CHILDHOOD PHOTO, PLACE IT HERE...

CHILDHOOD YEARS....

Where did you grow up as a child?
(house, location, town etc)

_____
_____
_____

Who was your best friend or your best friends as a child?

_____
_____

What was your favorite day of the week and why?

_____
_____
_____
_____

CHILDHOOD YEARS....

What was your favorite meal as a child?

___

What elementary/primary school did you attend and where was it located?

___

___

Describe your most memorable moment or story from elementary/primary school.

___

___

___

___

___

___

___

DO YOU HAVE ANY SCHOOL PHOTOS, OR OTHER DETAILS TO SHARE?

TEENAGE YEARS

TEENAGE YEARS....

Describe your dress sense and clothing as a teenager. Is there anything that stands out for you?

___

When and where did you learn to drive a vehicle?

___

What was your first vehicle and how much did you purchase it for? Tell us your special 'first car' story!

___

INCLUE ANY 'FIRST VEHICLE' PHOTOS OR OTHER INFORMATION HERE..

TEENAGE YEARS....

What High School did you attend and where was it located?

_____
_____
_____

Who was you favorite teacher or coach and why?

_____
_____
_____

What was your favorite subject at school?

_____
_____
_____

Did you date anyone at High School?

_____
_____
_____

SHARE ANY HIGH SCHOOL PHOTOS OR FURTHER DETAILS HERE

TEENAGE YEARS....

What hobbies did you have as a teenager?
_____
_____

What is your most memorable moment as a teenager?
_____
_____
_____
_____

If you knew what you know today, what would you have done differently as a teenager?
_____
_____
_____
_____

SHARE ANY PHOTOS OR OTHER DETAILS HERE

TEENAGE YEARS....

Did you have a close friendship group? Have you maintained contact with any of them?
_____
_____
_____
_____
_____

Did you have any nicknames at High School?
_____
_____

What 5 words come to mind to describe your teenage years?
1. _____
2. _____
3. _____
4. _____
5. _____

WHEN I WAS..

WHEN I WAS....

When I was a child, my mode of transport to school was..
_____
_____

When I was in my teens, the biggest news story that I recall was .....
_____
_____
_____

When I was growing up, my 3 favorite movies were:

1. _____
2. _____
3. _____

WHEN I WAS....

When I was a child, the first movie I went to the theatre to see was..

_____

When I graduated from elementary/primary school, the year was.. _____

When I was a child, I wanted to be a......

_____

When I was 18 years old, my favorite music and band was..

_____

When I was in my teens, the most popular thing to do on a Saturday night was.......

_____

_____

When I was young, I loved to travel to.......

_____

_____

_____

SHARE ANY FURTHER TRAVEL MEMORIES HERE..

PARENTHOOD

PARENTHOOD....

How old were you when you first became a parent?

___

Explain how you felt emotionally when you bacame a parent for the first time?

___

___

___

___

___

Where were you located (city/town/country) when you had your first child?

___

___

___

___

SHARE SOME PARENTING PHOTOS HERE..

PARENTHOOD....

What has been the biggest challenge for you as a parent?

_____
_____
_____
_____

What are 3 key responsibilities you believe are important as a parent?

1 _____

2 _____

3 _____

PARENTHOOD....

EXPAND ON ANY FURTHER PARENTING MEMORIES YOU MAY LIKE TO SHARE

"A mother's love is everything. It is what brings a child into this world. It is what molds their entire being. When a mother sees her child in danger, she is literally capable of anything. Mothers have lifted cars off of their children and destroyed entire dynasties. A mother's love is the strongest energy known to man."
—Jamie McGuire

MORE ABOUT ME!

MORE ABOUT ME.....

Not many people know this about me, so let me share it with you:

_____
_____
_____
_____
_____
_____
_____

The activity or hobby that I enjoy most to do now is.....

_____
_____

I have the unique ability to be able to....

_____
_____
_____

MORE ABOUT ME....

If I was able to go back to a special time in history, it would be...

___

If I could pass on one word of advice to others, it would be..

___

There are special moments in life that you wish you could pause to enjoy for longer. Mine would be......

___

MORE ABOUT ME....

I wish I had the opportunity to...
_____
_____
_____

The quote that resonates most with me is..
_____
_____
_____

My favorite book of all time is:
_____

If there is one thing I would like to be remembered for it would be:
_____
_____
_____

MORE ABOUT ME....

When I look back on my life so far, my 3 proudest moments are:

1 _____

2 _____

3 _____

If there were 3 famous people that I could invite for dinner they would be:

1 _____

2 _____

3 _____

MORE ABOUT ME.....

From my teen years, these are the jobs that I've had:

___
___
___
___
___
___
___
___
___
___

MORE ABOUT ME....

One of the jobs that stands out as my most enjoyable has been..

_____

_____

The most interesting place I have ever traveled to has been.... (include the year/date this occurred)

_____

_____

_____

If I was given a free return flight to anywhere in the world, I would visit...(include your 'Why')

_____

_____

_____

INCLUDE PHOTOS HERE..

FINAL NOTES

FINAL NOTES.....

There have been many questions that I have answered in this book, but I would also like to share this with you...

Your time to write anything else you wish to share...

FINAL NOTES....

FINAL NOTES....

FINAL NOTES....

USE THE FOLLOWING PAGES FOR CERTIFICATES, AWARDS. PHOTO'S ETC..

THANK YOU FOR SHARING YOUR LIFE STORY

This book was created by

Romney Nelson

OTHER BOOKS
BY
Romney Nelson and The Life Graduate Publishing Group

www.ingramcontent.com/pod-product-compliance
Lightning Source LLC
LaVergne TN
LVHW060143080526
838202LV00049B/4069